Planet Earth

Published in 2011 by Kingfisher
This edition published in 2013 by Kingfisher
an imprint of Macmillan Children's Books
a division of Macmillan Publishers Limited
20 New Wharf Road, London N1 9RR
Basingstoke and Oxford
Associated companies throughout the world
www.panmacmillan.com

ISBN 978-0-7534-3726-1

First published as *Kingfisher Young Knowledge: Planet Earth* in 2006
Additional material produced for Macmillan Children's Books by Discovery Books Ltd

Copyright © Macmillan Children's Books 2011

1 3 5 7 9 8 6 4 2
1SPL/0713/WKT/UTD/128MA

A CIP catalogue record for this book is available from the British Library.

Printed in China

Note to readers: the website addresses listed in this book are correct at the time of going to print.
However, due to the ever-changing nature of the internet, website addresses and content can
change. Websites can contain links that are unsuitable for children. The publisher cannot be held
responsible for changes in website addresses or content, or for information obtained through
a third party. We strongly advise that internet searches be supervised by an adult.

Acknowledgements
The publisher would like to thank the following for permission to reproduce their material. Every care has been taken
to trace copyright holders. However, if there have been unintentional omissions or failure to trace copyright holders,
we apologise and will, if informed, endeavour to make corrections in any future edition.
b = bottom, *c* = centre, *l* = left, *t* = top, *r* = right

Photographs: *Cover* Shutterstock/Atiketta Sangasaeng; Shutterstock/leonello calvetti; *Pages 2–3*
Photolibrary.com; 4–5 Corbis Clay Perry; 6 Getty Imagebank; 7 Getty Stone; 8*bl* Photolibrary.com;
8–9 Science Photo Library Roger Harris; 9*b* Photolibrary.com; 12*l* Corbis Rupak de Chowdhuri;
13*t* Photolibrary.com; 13*br* Getty Photodisc; 12–13 Science Photo Library Pekka Parvianen; 16–17 Getty
Imagebank; 16*cr* Photolibrary.com; 18*bl* Corbis NASA; 18–19 Getty Stone; 20–21 Corbis Tom Bean;
21*br* Getty AFP Yoshikazu Tsuno; 22–21 Corbis R.T. Holcomb; 23*tr* Corbis Charles & Josette Lenars;
24–25 Photolibrary.com; 24*c* Corbis Galen Rowell; 25*tl* Getty Stone; 26*l* Corbis Michael Freeman;
26–27 Getty Imagebank; 27*t* Photolibrary.com; 29 Corbis Audrey Gibson; 30–31 Getty Imagebank;
30*b* Corbis Robert Weight; 31*tr* Arcticphoto; 32–33 Corbis Yann Arthus-Bertrand; 32*bl* Frank Lane Picture
Agency Minden Pictures; 33*tl* Photolibrary.com; 34–35 Photolibrary.com; 34*tr* Frank Lane Picture Agency
Minden Pictures; 34*b* Getty Taxi; 35*bl* Corbis Craig Tuttle; 36-37 Frank Lane Picture Agency Minden
Pictures; 36*b* Getty Stone; 37*tr* Corbis Michael Yamashita; 38–39 Getty Digital Vision; 38*b* Getty Photodisc;
39*br* Corbis Tim Wright; 40–41 Getty Digital Vision; 40*bl* Getty Photodisc; 41*c* Getty Photodisc;
48*b* Shutterstock Images/Julien Grondin; 48*t* Shutterstock Images/Marino Bocelli; 49 Shutterstock
Images/kkaplin; 52*l* Shutterstock Images/Dmitry Naumov; 52*r* Shutterstock Images/Joao Virissimo;
53 Shutterstock Images/Chee-Onn Leong; 56 Shutterstock Images/Eduardo Rivero

Commissioned photography on pages 42–47 by Andy Crawford
Project-maker and photoshoot co-ordinator: Jo Connor
Thank you to models Alex Bandy, Alastair Carter, Tyler Gunning and Lauren Signist

Planet Earth

Deborah Chancellor

KINGFISHER

Contents

What is the Earth?

The Earth is a planet in space. It is one of eight planets that circle around the Sun in our Solar System. Seen from space, the Earth looks blue. This is because most of it is covered with oceans and seas.

Central America

The continents

The large areas of land are called continents. We can see the shape of the continents in photos taken from space. This continent is South America.

South America

The atmosphere

There is a blanket of gases around the Earth, called the atmosphere. White clouds swirl around in our planet's atmosphere.

atmosphere

Inside the Earth

The Earth is a rocky planet. It is divided into three main parts – the crust, the mantle and the core. We live on the crust, which is a thin layer of solid rock. Not far under our feet, the rock is so hot that it is liquid.

crust

The crust

In some places under the sea, the Earth's crust is only six kilometres thick. Under most of the land, the crust is about 35 kilometres thick.

The core

The core is the hottest part of the Earth. At its centre, temperatures can reach up to 5,000°C.

mantle

inner core

outer core

The mantle

The hot rock in the Earth's mantle melts to become liquid. We can see molten rock when a volcano erupts.

The water cycle

The world's water is never used up.
The Sun warms up sea water, turning
it to water vapour. This vapour rises
into the air, then comes down as rain.
The rain then flows back to the sea.
This is called the water cycle.

Sun heats sea water, making water vapour

water falls as rain

Water world

Most of the world's water is in the
oceans. Only one per cent of all
the world's water moves around
in the water cycle.

*water falls
as rain*

*water vapour
rises to form
clouds*

*water collects
in rivers and
flows to the sea*

Rain
Water vapour in clouds falls to the ground as rain. Some places get lots of rain. Mawsynram, in northern India, gets over 11 metres of rain every year. It is the wettest place in the world.

Weather and climate

Weather happens when the air around us changes. Air can be moving or still, hot or cold, wet or dry, or a mixture of these things. Water has a big part to play in the weather. Without it, there would be no clouds, rain or fog.

Tropical climate

The weather a place usually gets over a long time is called the climate. Climates vary in different parts of the world. In tropical places, the climate is hot and steamy.

Desert climate

In deserts, the climate is dry. On average, deserts have less than 2.5 centimetres of rain in a year. If all the rain comes at once, there are floods.

Trapping heat

Pollution in the air may trap some of the Sun's heat and stop it escaping back into space. As a result, climates all over the world may be changing and may become more extreme.

14 Clouds, rain and snow

Clouds are made of millions of tiny water droplets or ice crystals. Water droplets in clouds join together to make raindrops, and ice crystals combine to form snowflakes. Clouds come in many shapes and sizes.

Snow

Snowflakes usually melt on their way down to Earth. But if the air near the ground is freezing, we get snow.

Different clouds

Low stratus clouds can bring rain. Fluffy cumulus clouds are seen on sunny days. High, wispy cirrus clouds are made of ice.

cirrus cloud

cumulus cloud

Thunder clouds

Cumulonimbus clouds are the biggest clouds of all. Some are taller than Earth's highest mountain, Mount Everest! They bring heavy rain, thunder and lightning.

Wind

Wind is air that is moving around. It can be as gentle as a breeze, or as rough as a gale. Wind is made when the Sun warms the air to make it rise upwards. Cold air rushes in to fill the gap, making a wind blow.

When the wind blows

Wind travels at different speeds. A light breeze makes clouds drift across the sky. Stronger winds make trees sway, while very strong winds, called hurricanes, can cause lots of damage.

Air currents

Birds can glide along on rising currents of warm air. Seagulls hardly need to flap their wings to stay up high in the sky.

Hurricanes and tornadoes

Hurricanes and tornadoes are dangerous wind storms. Hurricanes form over the sea, and when they reach land they can cause terrible damage. Tornadoes are powerful whirlwinds that form over land.

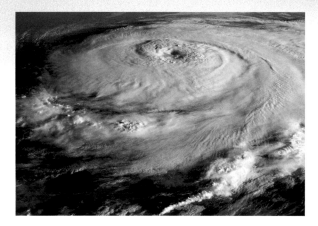

Hurricane
This satellite photo shows a hurricane in the Caribbean sea. It is heading for the coast of Florida, in the USA.

Twister

Tornadoes are also called twisters. Wind speed at the centre of a twister reaches up to 400 kilometres an hour – this is the fastest wind on Earth.

Earthquakes

An earthquake is a shaking or trembling of the Earth's surface caused by forces underground. Most earthquakes are too weak to be noticed, but strong ones can crack the ground and cause houses to fall down.

Fault zones

Most earthquakes happen at fault zones, where the plates that make up the Earth's crust push or slide against each other. This sends massive vibrations through the rock to shake the surface.

movement
of plate

Fault line

This huge crack in the ground is the San Andreas Fault, in California, USA. Two of the Earth's plates grind past each other here. They have caused some massive earthquakes.

Earthquake drill

Earthquakes are quite common in some places. In Japan, school children wear protective hats when practising what to do if there is an earthquake.

Volcanoes

A volcano is a mountain that was made from molten rock called lava. The lava comes from deep under the ground. During an eruption it forces its way up through a weak point in the Earth's crust. Volcanoes can erupt on land or deep under the ocean.

Inside a volcano

Molten rock, called magma, collects in a chamber. When the volcano erupts, magma is forced upwards, through a vent.

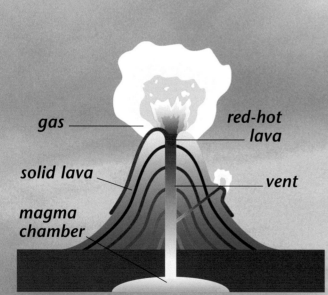

gas

red-hot lava

solid lava

vent

magma chamber

Bubbling mud

The land around volcanoes becomes very hot. Pools of mud or water bubble and boil on the Earth's surface.

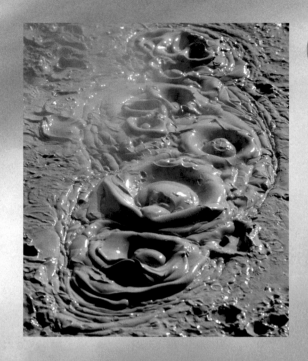

Giant volcano

The biggest active volcano in the world is in Hawaii. This lava flow is from the Mauna Ulu crater there.

Mountains

Mountains form over millions of years. They are made when two plates under the Earth's crust push together, forcing up huge folds of rock. As the mountain is pushed upwards, ice, wind and weather wear it down. This is called erosion.

The Alps

The Alps in Europe are a few million years old. Young mountains have jagged peaks. The weather has not had time to smooth down the sharp edges of rock.

The Himalayas

The 14 tallest mountains in the world are in the Himalayas, in Asia. These mountains are over 50 million years old.

Rivers and lakes

Most rivers carry water downhill to lakes or the sea. Some are so powerful they change the shape of the land they pass through. They carry rocks and mud along with them, cutting deep valleys and gorges as they go.

Lakes

Lakes are large areas of fresh water surrounded by land. Lakes are usually found in valley bottoms but they sometimes form in the craters of old volcanoes (left).

A river's journey

A river begins its journey in high ground, where it flows quickly downhill. When a river reaches flat ground it flows much more slowly and can sometimes form large bends called meanders.

Grand Canyon

The Colorado river in the USA has carved out the deepest gorge in the world. The fast-moving waters have worn away the rock to help create the amazing Grand Canyon.

The oceans

Oceans cover most of planet Earth. They are deeper in some parts than in others. This is because the ocean floor is not flat. There are mountains, valleys, plains and deep trenches under the sea.

Big blue sea

The five main oceans are the Arctic, Atlantic, Pacific, Indian and Southern oceans. The largest of these oceans is the Pacific.

volcano

deep trench

shipwreck

Low tide

At low tide, rockpools can be found on rocky beaches. The pools are covered over again at high tide.

Islands

Some underwater mountains and volcanoes are so tall, they rise above the surface of the water. Many islands are actually the tips of underwater mountains.

mountain range

island

30 The poles

The North Pole is in the middle of the Arctic ocean. This is a frozen ocean, surrounded by the world's most northern lands. The South Pole is at the heart of Antarctica. Most of this continent is covered with thick ice.

Antarctic science

Antarctica is the coldest and windiest continent. The only people who live there are scientists, who work in research stations.

Icebergs

In Antarctica and the Arctic, icebergs break away from ice sheets or glaciers and float in the icy ocean. We see only a tiny part of an iceberg – the rest is hidden under water.

Northern Lights

The Northern Lights, or aurora borealis, can be seen in northern Canada, Alaska and Scandinavia. The spectacular display takes place high up in the atmosphere.

Deserts

Deserts are the driest places on Earth, because it hardly ever rains. Some deserts are sandy, and others are rocky. Some are very hot, while others are freezing cold in winter.

Desert plants

Cactus plants grow in American deserts. They can live for a long time without rain, because they store water in their thick stems. Some birds make their homes in cactus stems.

Wind erosion

Deserts can be windy places. Wind blasts sand at tall rocks, gradually wearing them away. The rocks in Monument Valley, USA, show how wind can change the landscape in a desert.

Biggest desert

The Sahara, in northern Africa, is the biggest desert in the world. It contains the world's tallest sand dunes, which are up to 430 metres high and five kilometres long.

Forests

A forest is a large area of land covered in trees. About a fifth of the world is covered with forest. In the past, forests grew over much more of the planet, but people have cut many of the trees down.

Deciduous

Trees that lose leaves in the winter are called deciduous. The leaves change colour and fall off the trees in the autumn.

Rainforest

Rainforests grow in hot
countries where there is
a lot of rain. The wettest
rainforests have over ten
metres of rainfall a year.

Evergreen

Big forests of evergreen trees
grow in northern parts of the
world. Evergreen trees do not
lose their leaves in winter.
Their branches slope down,
so the snow slides off them.

Life on Earth

Earth may be the only planet in the universe that can support life. Our planet's oxygen and the water in its oceans are vital for living things to survive.

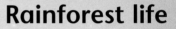

Rainforest life

There are many millions of types, or species, of animals and plants on Earth. Tropical rainforests are home to more than half of the world's plant and animal species.

When life began

Scientists believe that life on Earth began over 3.5 billion years ago. It has been slowly changing, or evolving, ever since. Remains of ancient creatures tell us a lot about life a very long time ago.

In the sea

The oceans were home to the world's first animals. Some ocean species, such as sea turtles, are over 200 million years old.

Earth's riches

Many of the Earth's natural riches are hidden deep under the ground. Fossil fuels, such as oil and gas, are found in rocks, thousands of metres below the Earth's surface. They are made from the remains of ancient plants and animals.

Minerals

Rocks are made from minerals. Rare minerals, such as the diamonds and rubies in this crown, are called gems.

Oil and gas

Oil and gas are fossil fuels, which are pumped up from holes drilled into the Earth's crust. They are found in places that are, or once were, under the sea.

Coal

Coal is a fossil fuel that is burned in huge amounts to make electricity. It is dug out from deep underground mines.

Looking after the Earth

The Earth gives us food, water and air to breathe. Sadly, people have not looked after it, and many places are now polluted. Lots of plants and animals have died out, or soon will do. We must all help make the Earth a cleaner place.

Saving forests

Trees help keep the air clean, and provide shelter for many different animals. People must stop cutting down so many forests, and plant more trees.

Recycling

We can make new things from old materials. This is called recycling. Bottles, cans, paper, plastic and aluminium foil can all be recycled.

New energy

Scientists are developing new forms of energy that do not pollute. Many of the forces of nature, such as the wind, can be used to make electricity.

Make a volcano

Understanding eruptions

There are about 1,500 active volcanoes in the world today. When a volcano erupts, huge underground pressures force liquid rock up into the air. You can make your own volcano with some simple materials. In your volcano, sodium bicarbonate mixes with vinegar to make carbon dioxide gas.

Using the clay, make a hollow volcano and place it on the tray. Slide the plastic bottle inside.

You will need
- Modelling clay
- Baking tray
- Small, plastic bottle with the top sliced off
- Sodium bicarbonate
- Funnel
- Vinegar
- Red food colouring

Half fill the bottle with sodium bicarbonate. You may need to use the funnel for this.

Place your volcano and baking tray on a flat surface. You can take it outside if you prefer.

Mix the vinegar with the food colouring. Pour them into the bottle using the funnel.

Stand back and watch your volcano erupt!

Make a rain gauge

Measuring rain

There is an easy way to measure how much rain falls during a shower. Put your rain gauge out in the open. When the shower is over, open the lid and collect the rain water in a measuring jug. Note down how much rain fell.

You will need

- Large plastic bottle
- Scissors
- Elastic bands
- Garden pole or stick
- Measuring jug
- Pen and paper

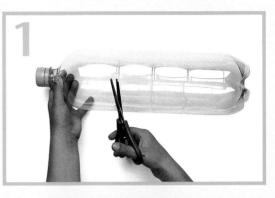

Cut a section off the plastic bottle, using the scissors. You may need to ask an adult to help you.

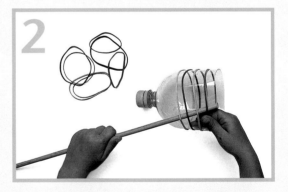

Put elastic bands around the bottle. Slide the pole under the bands and position the bottle with the screw cap facing down, to catch any raindrops.

Make a **windmill**

Spinning sails
You cannot see the wind, but you can watch what it does. Make a windmill and see how the wind blows it around.

You will need
- 2 squares of coloured card
- Pencil and ruler
- Scissors and sticky tape
- Drawing pins and wooden rod

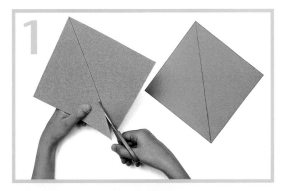

Draw a line across each card square, from one corner to the other. Cut along this line to make two triangles.

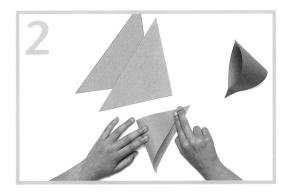

You will now have four triangles. Fold each of the triangles in half, fixing the corners together with sticky tape.

Place the corners of the four triangles on top of each other. Ask an adult to help you pin them on to the wooden rod.

Forest habitat

Make your own forest

The place in which an animal lives is called a habitat. Everything an animal needs to survive can be found in its habitat, for example, food and shelter. There are many different kinds of animal habitat on Earth. You can make a model of a forest habitat with craft materials.

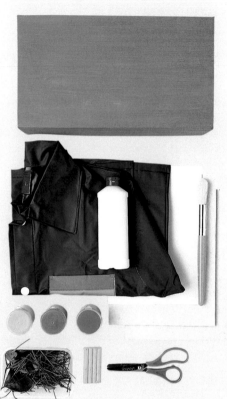

tree template to draw around

You will need
- Big shoebox
- Poster paints and brush
- Pencil
- Tracing paper
- Card
- Scissors
- Glue
- Modelling clay
- Plant material – leaves, grass or twigs
- Toy forest animals

1

Paint inside your shoebox, using brown paint for the ground, green for the grass and blue for the sky.

2

Use the template on the opposite page to draw some trees on card. Cut out the plant shapes.

3

Paint the trees. When they are dry, fix them inside the box with glue or clay. Scatter the plant material on the ground and arrange your animals in their new home.

Glossary

Atmosphere – the air around the Earth

Cactus – a plant that can grow in places with little rain

Crust – the layer of rock around the Earth

Currents – movements of air or water in a particular direction

Drill – a repeated practice or exercise

Droplets – very small drops of liquid

Eruption – the pouring out of hot, molten rock from a volcano

Fault – a break in the Earth's crust

Gas – a substance that is not a solid or a liquid. Air is a mixture of gases

Glaciers – moving rivers of ice

Gorges – valleys with steep sides

Ice crystals – tiny pieces of ice

Magma – molten rock underground

Mineral – a hard natural substance that makes up rocks

Oxygen – one of the gases in the air

Plates – the Earth's crust is made up of about 12 large plates

Polluted – made dirty by waste substances

Pollution – harmful waste that damages the environment

Rainforest – a dense forest of tall trees that grows in a tropical area

Sand dunes – big hills of sand that are formed by the wind

Satellite photo – a photograph taken from a satellite orbiting the Earth

Solar System – the planets that orbit the Sun

Trenches – long, narrow valleys

Tropical – belonging to the tropics – an area around the equator with hot, wet weather

Valleys – areas of low land between hills or mountains

Vapour – a mass of tiny water droplets in the air

Whirlwind – a strong wind in a tight spiral

This book includes material that would be particularly useful in helping to teach children aged 7–11 elements of the English and Science curricula and some cross-curricular lessons involving Geography and Art.

Extension activities

Reading
Scan the book to find countries or oceans (Now find them on an atlas. Pages 6, 18, 21, 25, 27, 28, 30, 31, 33).

Writing
Imagine you are an alien reporting on planet Earth. Use this book to find six facts or topics that you would put in your report. Now write it.

Use the information about the water cycle (pages 10–11) to write the story of a raindrop from falling to rising up again.

Write a story or poem that shows what it is like to be caught in a twister (page 19), earthquake (pages 20–21) or volcano eruption (page 22).

Speaking and listening
Find the information on very hot or cold places in the world. Prepare a one-minute presentation to a group explaining why they are hot or cold.

Science
In addition to the topic of planet Earth (all pages) this book will help with the topics of rocks and soils (pages 8–9, 20–21, 22–23, 24–25, 33 and 38–39) and habitats (pages 24, 26, 28–29, 30–31, 32, 34–35 and 36). Children could choose two or three habitats and compare their environments and wildlife.

Look at pages 10–11 and draw your own labelled poster or diagram of the water cycle.

Cross-curricular links
Geography: (See reading task on using an atlas.) This book links

with the topic of weather (pages 12–19), rivers and seas (pages 10–11, 26–27, 28–29, 31), islands (page 29) and environmental issues (pages 6, 13, 36, 38–39, 40–41).

History: Page 37 says when life began. Find an animal from the past and try to find out how it changed (evolved). For example, you could investigate *Hyracotherium*, an ancestor of the horse.

Art and design: Look at page 14. Make your own snowflakes by folding paper and cutting through the layers to make a pattern.

Using the projects
Children can follow or adapt these projects at home. Here are some ideas for extending them:

Pages 42–43: Create a landscape for your volcano and see how the eruption changes it.

Page 44: Keep a record of your rain measurements for a month. When did it rain most or least? Make a bar or line graph to show the rainfall for the month.

Page 45: Can you make a windmill that shows the direction of the wind?

Page 46: There is information on different types of forest on pages 34–35. Make a model of one of them, showing the different layers.

Did you know?

- The Earth is more than 4.5 billion years old.

- Seventy per cent of the Earth's surface is covered in water.

- The largest recorded earthquake in the world was in Chile on 22 May 1960. It measured 9.5 on the Richter scale.

- The world's longest mountain range is the Andes in South America. It stretches 7,200 kilometres from north to south.

- Over 16 million thunderstorms take place across the world each year.

- The largest cactus in the world is the saguaro cactus. Some cacti have been known to reach 14 metres in height.

- The highest mountain in the world is Mount Everest in the Himalayas. It is 8,850 metres tall.

- The Earth's crust varies in thickness under land but it is generally between 30 and 50 kilometres thick.

- The longest river in the world is the Nile, in Africa. It is 6,650 kilometres long.

- Antarctica is the coldest place on Earth. Temperatures as low as −89°C have been recorded.

- One in ten of the known animal species in the world live in the Amazon rainforest.

- There are at least 1,500 active volcanoes around the world.

- The Californian redwood is the tallest species of tree in the world. It can grow to over 100 metres tall.

- The driest place on Earth is Arica in Chile, where as little as 0.76 millimetres of rain falls in a year.

- The world's largest ocean is the Pacific, covering 169.2 million square kilometres.

- The Earth is 12,756 kilometres in diameter.

- The Grand Canyon (below), in the United States, is the largest canyon on Earth, reaching a depth of over 1.8 kilometres.

Planet Earth quiz

The answers to these questions can all be found by looking back through the book. See how many you get right. You can check your answers on page 56.

1) Where can the world's biggest active volcano be found?
A – Holland
B – Hawaii
C – Haiti

2) What is underground molten rock called?
A – Magma
B – Lava
C – Crust

3) How hot can the Earth's core get?
A – 1,000°C
B – 3,000°C
C – 5,000°C

4) What are trees that lose their leaves in winter called?
A – Deciduous
B – Conifers
C – Evergreen

5) What are the gases that form a blanket around the Earth called?
A – Clouds
B – The atmosphere
C – The Solar System

6) How old are the Himalayan mountains?
A – 50 million years
B – 50,000 years
C – 500 years

7) Which of the deserts is the largest on Earth?
A – The Gobi Desert
B – The Sahara Desert
C – The Arabian Desert

8) Where are hurricanes formed?
A – Over the sea
B – Over mountains
C – Over desert

9) What speed can the wind at the centre of a tornado reach?
A – 40 kilometres an hour
B – 400 kilometres an hour
C – 4000 kilometres an hour

10) Who are the only people that live in Antarctica?
A – Astronomers
B – Miners
C – Scientists

11) What percentage of the world's water moves around in the water cycle?
A – 1 per cent
B – 10 per cent
C – 100 per cent

12) When do scientists believe that life on Earth began?
A – 3,500 years ago
B – 3.5 million years ago
C – 3.5 billion years ago

Find out more

Books to read

Explorers: Planet Earth by Daniel Gilpin, Kingfisher, 2011

Flip the Flaps Planet Earth by Mike Goldsmith, Kingfisher, 2010

Guide to the Planet (Planet Earth) by Steve Murrie and Matthew Murrie, Scholastic Inc., 2009

Navigators: Planet Earth by Barbara Taylor, Kingfisher, 2009

Planet Earth by Katie Daynes, Usborne Publishing Ltd, 2008

Water Cycle (Planet Earth) by Amy Bauman, TickTock Books, 2008

The World's Oceans (Amazing Planet Earth) by Terry Jennings, Franklin Watts, 2009

Places to visit

Eden Project

www.edenproject.com

The Eden Project in Cornwall has a huge amount of things to see including three enormous bio-domes, each with a different environment inside. There are a number of activities to participate in, which both children and adults will enjoy.

The Living Rainforest

www.livingrainforest.org

The Living Rainforest in Berkshire, UK, has more than 700 species of animals and plants for visitors to observe, including giant water lilies and the West African dwarf crocodile.

Our Dynamic Earth

www.dynamicearth.co.uk/home

Our Dynamic Earth in Edinburgh, Scotland, has a wealth of exhibitions and attractions including a journey through the centre of the Earth, a look back over the last 15,000 million years of the Earth's history and a trip into the deep oceans.

Websites

CBBC Newsround: Volcanoes

news.bbc.co.uk/cbbcnews/hi/find_out/ guides/tech/volcanoes/newsid_1768000/ 1768595.stm

This website has lots of exciting information about volcanoes including why volcanoes erupt, where they can be found and the effect a volcanic eruption can have on the surrounding environment.

Met Office Education

www.metoffice.gov.uk/education/kids/ weather_words_weatherforecast.html

On the Met Office education website you can find out all about the many aspects of the weather. There is information about the water cycle, a variety of games and activities, and a guide to making your own weather station.

BBC Schools Rivers and Coasts

www.bbc.co.uk/schools/riversandcoasts/ rivers/whatis_river/index.shtml

On this website you will learn about rivers and coasts, how rivers form and how they change the shape of the land they flow through.

Planet Earth
quiz answers

1) B	7) B
2) A	8) A
3) C	9) B
4) A	10) C
5) B	11) A
6) A	12) C